# A $ Year Federal Budget Improvement for the US

# Author – Karl Guenther

# <u>Dedications to:</u>

To the Lower and Middle Classes of the
United States

## Table Summaries

# Table of Contents

# Contents

Table of Contents

Table of Contents

# Table of Tables Including Hyperlink Reference Tables

Table of Tables Including Hyperlink Reference
Tables

# Chapter 1:

# Introduction

## 1.0 Key Related Points

- **There is a lot of potential improvement in the federal government's budgeting of the United States. That is especially true for things related to healthcare costs.**
- **Much of the improvement here in this book can be a joint effort to improve the financial position of the lower and middle classes.**
- **Many of the improvements can also improve the health of the people of the United States and the world.**
- **The dramatic cuts to the medical industry proposed do a lot to reduce costs to individuals and allow even more significant cuts to federal medical costs.**

# 1.1 Opening Remarks

The new administration of the United States in early 2025 is planning to work on sizeable budget cuts. This book adds to that work in a way that aligns with my thinking on some things that need to be done. These ideas can augment or add to budget planning. My additions to government planning here on the budget will likely take up to 25 years to work through. However, I could see about two-thirds of the medical cost reduction and benefits within five years. We should plan to work towards a $2 trillion annual budget improvement within 5 years and the whole $3 trillion improvement within 25 years.

My ideas add a primary medical industry and government economic change in a way that helps the lower and middle classes. This work is also in addition to my work on publishing a book titled "Vaccines – Scientific Analysis – And the $7.8 Trillion Per Year Economic Opportunity for the United States: A Strategy and Reference Book R3.

One significant problem with the finances of those not in the upper class or higher end of the middle class of the United States is medical and insurance costs related to medical needs.

My general ideas are as follows as to how we get to a $3 Trillion federal budget improvement over 25 years and to a $2 trillion one over 5 years, takes into account the following:

Chapter 1:   Introduction

- An expectation that the new administration, starting in early 2025, will be able to reduce federal spending by about $1 to $2 trillion per year but will offset all of the spending cuts with tax cuts, primarily for the upper class. My view is that the lower and middle classes will get some benefit from the changes but not anywhere as much as they deserve.
- This book is about a future change to the early 2025-2026 planning to tilt the planning in favor of the lower and middle classes, increasing the budget improvement to $3 trillion over 25 years. A $2 trillion budget cut over five years is only applicable if the new administration changes its planning to do more to tilt planning away from the significant improvements tailored to the upper class.

# 1.2 Analysis of 2024 Budget and Opportunities

The most significant budget opportunities are:

- A permanent fix to the budgetary concerns related to Social Security
- Efforts to reduce and improve the cost and functionality of the medical industry – See Chapters 2 to 4
- Reductions and improvements in the spending for defense – See Chapter 5, Section 5.2
- Other non-discretionary parts of the federal budget – See Chapter 5, Section 5.3

Chapter 1:   Introduction

As I see things, the most significant financial opportunity for federal budget improvements I am working on in this book is a dramatic change in how the federal government manages and directs the medical industry.

When I say manages and directs in many ways, I believe the government does not need to override how medical doctors write prescriptions and manage patient care but augment things in many ways. For example, when a prescription is written for one year, the interactive AI process for extending the end of a prescription could override things at the pharmacy involved.

My thinking is an additional cut to spending by the Federal government that adds up to about $3 trillion per year over a 25-year time frame, including the following.

1. About $200 billion out of the defense budget by using lower-cost drone technology and fewer expensive submarines and planes and such
2. About $800 billion out of federal medical expense which is currently at about $2 trillion a year.
3. About a $2 trillion reduction of spending as worked by Elon Musk, Trump, and others

Please note that the above will be discussed more in Chapter 5 and includes what is called the Cato report,

Chapter 1:   Introduction

from a Washington, D.C., Libertarian think tank group.

Improvements in health and reductions in medical costs have the most dramatic effect on job opportunities for individuals and on financial improvements for the lower and much of the middle class.

Please note that the new Department of Government Efficiency and my proposal in this book overlap, and it may be harder to achieve the complete budget improvement. But with some hard work, I believe the bulk of the improvements can be achieved.

# 1.3 A Permanent Fix for Costs of Social Security

The Social Security age for full benefits should adjust automatically from year to year under a scheme that considers average longevity so that there are no major budgetary problems.

# Chapter 2 Use of AI, Artificial Intelligence in Medicine and Government

## 2.0 Key Related Points

- **The use of AI, artificial intelligence, can be a driving force in government and the medical industry to reduce medical and government costs dramatically.**
- **One example of AI use is to have many prescriptions filled, in many cases, using AI and online and cell phone apps rather than a doctor's visit.**

- **Doctor's visits should be reserved for cases when a doctor's experience is really needed.**
- **Video conference apps for online meetings with doctors and nurse practitioners should be developed and used. Special equipment should be designed to assist with the video conference setup.**
- **Online systems for interactions with medical practitioners should be developed to reduce the number of in-person visits with medical professionals.**

## 2.1 Introductory Comments

With the advent of AI being used in more ways in our society, we can now look forward to its use in interactions related to various aspects of medical care. Doctors' visits should be reserved for when they are needed. Many interactions related to ongoing medical activities currently requiring a visit to a doctor's office should be eliminated and done via cell phones or other online interactions. The medical charges related to these activities should be a small percentage of today's medical billing.

Chapter 2 Use of AI, Artificial Intelligence in Medicine and Government

The idea is that the design of the new medical system should be done by the government and requirements to reduce costs to the patients and the government significantly. The government is in an ideal position to do this because of the medical-related money now paid from government revenues.

## 2.2 Use of AI in Prescription Drug Renewals

The patients and medical doctors should have some say in the schedule of prescription drug renewals, but the AI system should also review the schedules. The idea is that AI would review the schedule and help set it to a more reasonable time frame. The schedule should not be set to help increase the finances of the doctor's medical practices involved. Of course, the schedule would be different if addictive pain medicines were involved. There should be some feedback system and medical reviews that do not involve doctors in many cases. This would be where various patient medical readings like blood pressure testing can be done in many cases, such as in a pharmacy kiosk, without labor costs involved. In this case, the kiosk would interact with the AI involved and sometimes recommend or direct the patient to a medical doctor visit and schedule the visit.

Many temporary multitarget antivirals and antibacterials for illnesses like measles should only require AI online interactions via cell phone or a similar process.

Chapter 2 Use of AI, Artificial Intelligence in Medicine and Government

## 2.3 Greater Use of Video Teleconferencing and Phone Calls

Sometimes, video teleconferencing or a phone follow-up could be arranged to handle more patient-to-medical industry interactions. These types of intermediate reviews would be designed to lower the cost involved. AI interactions would also monitor and arrange this type of medical review when necessary or advisable.

AI Bots would be used to monitor patients' well-being. The system would also select people for cost and health tracking. Private data would be kept secret, and averages would be rolled up.

## 2.4 AI Bots and Tracking Plus Cell Phone Apps

Generally, we should allow anyone to be included in various groups of people who track their actual medical outcomes and costs versus the average actual outcome. I suggest the use of cell phone and other apps for those interested in tracking their results versus others. The main database of information would still remain on government computers, but individuals could track their relative position health-wise and cost-wise versus others.

We should also have AI reviews of doctors' health and cost-wise performance regarding their patients' results. Actual outcomes should drive part of the payment schedule for medical industry workers and their businesses.

# 2.5 Testing Techniques for State of Health With AI

In general, we could use a new set of testing hardware and applications integrated into the AI infrastructure being developed. This includes newer cholesterol level-checking equipment, blood pressure monitoring, and overall health monitoring and testing of people's overall health.

The emphasis should be more on individuals' self-reliance to monitor their health. This would be well integrated into AI infrastructure and cell phone and other computer applications.

Chapter 2 Use of AI, Artificial Intelligence in Medicine and Government

# Chapter 3 Other Changes to the Medical Industry

## 3.0 Key Related Points

- The US healthcare industry is way too expensive, and there should be about a 65% cut in the industry's cost.
- A set of activities should be worked on to reduce medical costs dramatically in all aspects of medicine.
- More at-home services should be provided for people needing medical assistance with a lower potential for hospital-acquired infections.

- **There should be a nutritionist involved in the life of all people early and often in life.**
- **Budget cuts of about 20% or more should done to most government health agencies, with about an 80% budget cut to the CDC.**
- **Polio is a virus easily handled by testing and multitarget antivirals.**

# 3.1 Introduction, Optimal Use of Nutritionists, and Dietary Changes

A bad diet is one of the most significant contributors to bad health, especially as one ages. So, diet should be reviewed early in adolescence or earlier, especially when consuming too much protein and sugar. Parents should also be better educated on the importance of a proper diet for themselves and their children. There should also be several additional times in the lives of adults when nutritionists and others review diet and healthy behavior. That includes activities like exercising and staying away from cigarettes.

The government, the medical industry, and society should also do a better job of striving for a healthier lifestyle for all.

Lower Chronic illness rates, better nutritional
activities, and personal exercise routines should
improve health, extend the time between doctor visits,
and reduce health-related costs. AI-related interaction
on cell phones or other apps should be a major part of
daily routines

A newly revamped medical industry and government
involvement in improving health should focus on
dramatically reducing chronic and neurological and
immune system illnesses.

We need more Alzheimer's studies and research to
find causes and resolutions

# 3.2 Development of New Treatments and Prevention for Pneumonia

Pneumonia is the primary cause of death as illnesses
get out of hand in the human body. This topic relates
to diseases like Measles, Pertussis, Whooping Cough,
etc. Unlike many other illnesses, we can provide a
means of preventing Pneumonia without using
vaccines.

I suggest developing antiviral capabilities for all
virus-related enzymes and a follow-up regimen to
address potential Pneumonia associated with viral
infections. It also looks very probable that strong
antibiotic alternatives can be on the horizon for

bacterial-based Pneumonia. Another thing to do is to work up multitarget antivirals. I don't mean two different viral-related enzymes, but each antiviral agent would have an enzyme inhibitor and another mechanism for fighting specific viruses or sets of viruses. Say, for example, a mechanism to capture and eliminate viruses from the body. Or, say, two or more antiviral-related inhibitors that are not both enzyme inhibitors.

In the case of bacterial infections, the medical community could develop monoclonal antibody treatments and other antibody-type treatments. One idea here would be the development of fast processing to gear up the creation of antibody treatments designed specifically for blood type and other specific human traits. Development could be fast-tracked at local pharmacies.

Other means to treat later-stage viral and bacterial infections could be engineered, developed, and tested. The treatment would be in line with my view that natural immunity will let the human immune system take down infections on its own in most cases. The later-stage viral and bacterial infection treatments would only be applied when close to being necessary. Some exceptions to this general thinking would be in cases where things are more sensitive in the middle stages of a more serious infection, like neurological infections.

# 3.3 Reduce or Eliminate the Use of Vaccines

Generally, I will accept the argument that considerable evidence in the vaccinated vs. unvaccinated studies warrants the elimination of vaccines or vaccine mandates. I have a robust scientific preference for eliminating all vaccine usage.

Vaccine usage leaves many families in a poor financial state for life because of things like ADHD, Autism, and learning disorders with reduced ability to earn a decent living.

# 3.4 Greater Use of Pharmacy Nurses and Kiosks

Changes at pharmacies to provide low-cost alternatives to mainline medical practices could be instrumental in reducing costs. Pharmacy kiosks would substantially contribute to society's improvements in reduced human suffering and potentially large cost cuts. I see a whole new tier of control over prescription drug control where it is easier for people to get what they need faster and at a lower cost. Allow some prescription drug permissions via online application processing and make more drugs available over the counter. For example, if a child has Measles and is five days into the illness, allow a parent to request an antiviral for

Measles for the child with only an AI process for
approval, like in Chapter 2, Section 2.2 above.

This same process would apply to many related
processes for other illnesses without a doctor's
approval.

A pharmacy nurse or a doctor would monitor the AI
application for abuse and get involved when overuse
is a potential problem. The nurse or doctor will
redirect the application process if overuse is
suspected and unjustified. So, part of the plan is to
reduce the use of expensive doctors and to provide a
more convenient and lower-cost process for people
who are ill in some cases and for treating child
illnesses where warranted.

Part of the idea here would be to have pharmacy
kiosks with low staffing requirements for
convenience and lower costs.

# **3.5 Development Of Antivirals For Every Enzyme Associated With Every Known Virus**

Antivirals have been developed for COVID-19 and
have been effective. They can be even more effective
when two or more target antiviral agents are involved.
Various viruses depend on different enzymes. So, we
should create different antivirals for all known
enzymes required for viruses to do the various things
they do. The idea of two target antivirals is to add a

second mechanism to antivirals that further reduces the capabilities of viruses. Researchers can explore expanding this concept further, reducing viruses' capabilities, and potentially developing methods to capture and eliminate viruses from the human or animal body.  We need to work on multitarget antivirals with three or more active agents and get up close to 99.8% efficacy for the antiviral package. The antiviral package should also provide extremely high flexibility as to when the antiviral can be administered and still be highly effective.

The slow process of getting antivirals tested and authorized is one of the biggest problems in dealing with the COVID-19 pandemic. At the same time, vaccine development was a high priority—Vaccines should never have been created for COVID-19. The virus mutated rapidly, and we expected typical vaccine side effects. We could have saved hundreds of thousands of lives. We could have reduced the cost of the COVID-19 pandemic to about 2% of what it was, with a much lesser impact on people. We should have developed effective antivirals about 50 years ago. And vaccine development should have come to an end around the same time.

# **3.6 Develop What I Call Multitarget Antivirals**

I discussed this in section 3.5 but will expand on it here. Multitarget antivirals should target viral-required enzymes, flush viruses out of the body quickly, and use other advanced methods.

We should have more viral capabilities targeted to augment the primary enzyme treatment. The second and additional target capabilities could even be more sophisticated, like the ability to flush viruses out of the body. The work would be incredibly advantageous. We could eliminate virtually all complications from childhood viral illnesses and other viral illnesses. And, I don't see the job of making this happen as all that expensive relative to the problems with vaccines or being challenging to achieve. Here is one article on various types of antivirals in **Hyperlink Reference Table 3.6-1 Seven classes of antiviral agents**.

*Table 1 - Hyperlink Reference Table 3.6-1 Seven classes of antiviral agents*

https://www.ncbi.nlm.nih.gov/pmc/articles/PMC9701656/#:~:text=Here%2C%20we%20briefly%20reviewed%207,polymers%2C%20and%20antiviral%20small%20molecules.

| See the Hyperlink above this table. | Google search: nih PMC9701656 |
|---|---|
| Title: Seven classes of antiviral agents | Authors: Aleksandr Ianevski,[1] Shahzaib Ahmad,[1] Kraipit Anunnitipat,[1] Valentyn Oksenych,[1] Eva Zusinaite,[2] Tanel |

| | |
|---|---|
| | Tenson,[2] Magnar Bjørås,[1] and Denis E. Kainov☒[1,2,3]<br><br>Published Online 11/27/2022 |
| **Book Summary of Link: The web page details each class of antiviral agents.**<br><br>**We should create multitarget antivirals that achieve about 99.8% efficacy and can be used at any point in an infection.** | Quoted Text: "Here, we briefly reviewed 7 classes of antiviral agents: neutralizing antibodies, neutralizing recombinant soluble human receptors, antiviral CRISPR/Cas systems, interferons, antiviral peptides, antiviral nucleic acid polymers, and antiviral small molecules." |

# 3.7 Also, Develop Ways To Do The Same for Other Pathogens

For all other bacterial and non-viral agents of illnesses, we should look at the same multitarget capability shown above. Again, I don't see the job of making this happen as all that expensive relative to the problems with vaccines or being challenging to achieve. Here are a couple of articles on antibacterial agents and alternatives to antibiotics. One reference is in **Hyperlink Reference Table 3.7-1 Bacterial Enzyme**, and the second is in **Hyperlink Reference**

**Table 3.7-2 Alternatives to Conventional
Antibiotics in the Era of Antimicrobial Resistance**.


*Table 2- Hyperlink Reference Table 3.7-1 Bacterial
Enzyme*

https://www.sciencedirect.com/topics/pharmacology-toxicology-and-pharmaceutical-science/bacterial-enzyme

| See the Hyperlink above this table. | Google search: Sciencedirect Bacterial Enzyme |
|---|---|
| Title: Bacterial Enzyme | Authors: Ghazaleh Laliani, Amir Avan<br><br>Published Online 2020 |
| Book Summary of Link: Several ways exist to inhibit bacterial growth using bacterial enzymes. | Quoted Text: "Given the different metabolic pathways that bacteria use for growth and pathogenesis, bacteria are capable of producing and secreting a wide range of enzymes that can function in many catalytic reactions. Numerous studies have shown that essential amino acids are vital for cellular metabolism and normal cell growth; hence, these |

| | |
|---|---|
| | amino acids can be a restricting factor in rapid growth conditions like tumor cell growth." |

*Table 3- Hyperlink Reference Table 3.7-2 Alternatives to Conventional Antibiotics in the Era of Antimicrobial Resistance*

| | |
|---|---|
| https://www.cell.com/trends/microbiology/abstract/S0966-842X(18)30286-5 | Google search: cell.com Alternatives Antibiotics Antimicrobial Resistance |
| Title: Alternatives to Conventional Antibiotics in the Era of Antimicrobial Resistance | Authors: Chandradhish Ghosh[1] · Paramita Sarkar[1] · Rahaf Issa[2] · Jayanta Haldar[1]  Published Online 4/2019 |
| **Book Summary of Link: This is an interesting article with some key ideas on dealing with antibiotic resistance and quitting vaccines.** | Quoted Text: "As bacteria grow resistant to conventional antibiotics, alternatives are being investigated, including antibodies, probiotics, bacteriophages, and antimicrobial peptides currently undergoing clinical trials.  The specificity of antibodies, and the |

| | inability of bacteria to develop resistance against them, make antibodies attractive, albeit expensive, alternative therapeutic agents. |
| | Bacteriophages have been used for therapy in some parts of the world. |
| | Antimicrobial peptides have long been considered as potential replacements for antibiotics but with limited success. Synthetic peptides and synthetic membrane-active agents might herald a shift." |

# 3.8 Development of Other Advanced Treatments for Illness

I mentioned this above in general, but an antiviral treatment for Measles-like viruses is already in the works. Still, the main thing with Measles and Bordetella Pertussis and a few other childhood illnesses is the ability to treat non-pneumococcal Pneumonia. Since advanced bacterial or viral infections typically cause these types of Pneumonia, medical treatments are needed to reduce the specific higher bacterial or viral counts in some manner. I believe these treatments could include advanced antibiotics or antivirals that can better treat advanced illnesses of these types. One other type of treatment would be advanced breathing treatments.

One advanced treatment, expanded use of Ivermectin, could have been used much more during the COVID-19 pandemic. Below is a write-up on potential use for cancer in **Hyperlink Reference Table 3.8-1 Ivermectin, a potential anticancer drug derived from an antiparasitic drug.**

*Table 4- Hyperlink Reference Table 3.8-1 Ivermectin, a potential anticancer drug derived from an antiparasitic drug*

| https://www.sciencedirect.com/science/article/pii/S1043661820315152 | Google search: Sciencedirect Ivermectin cancer |
|---|---|
| Title: Ivermectin, a potential anticancer drug derived from an antiparasitic drug | Authors: Mingyang Tang Xiaodong Hu, Yi Wang, Xin Yao, Wei Zhang, Chenying Yu, Fuying Cheng, Jiangyan Li, Qiang Fang<br><br>Published Online 1/2021 |
| **Book Summary of Link: Ivermectin shows real potential in the fight against Cancer.** | Quoted Text: "Highlights<br> • •<br>Ivermectin effectively suppresses the |

|  | proliferation and metastasis of cancer cells and promotes cancer cell death at doses that are nontoxic to normal cells. |
|  | • • |
|  | Ivermectin shows excellent efficacy against conventional chemotherapy drug-resistant cancer cells and reverses multidrug resistance." |

Here are some key highlights from that link:
"Ivermectin effectively suppresses the proliferation and metastasis of cancer cells and promotes cancer cell death at doses that are nontoxic to normal cells. Ivermectin is effective against conventional chemotherapy drug-resistant cancer cells and reverses multidrug resistance."

We must develop another critical category of medications for illnesses that cause brain swelling or Encephalitis.

# **3.9 The Development Of Dynamic AI-Assisted Ways To Quickly Build Antibody Therapies**

For any sickness when, the human immune system can't handle the disease within a reasonable amount of time, a local pharmacy could quickly produce tailored antibody treatments for customers within half an hour

Since antibody generation is a primary response of immune systems, generating applicable antibodies to assist in advanced infections could be a primary technique to apply. So, quickly generating applicable antibodies would be a great way to treat advanced infections that the immune system does not seem to be warding off on its own.

# 3.10 Work To Find The Root Causes Of All Illnesses

We use excessive amounts of money for vaccine development despite serious problems. Vaccines don't play well with the human immune system, and will never do so

I view the use of vaccines as a lazy cop-out by the medical industry and the government. We need to do much more for illnesses in general, especially diseases that vaccines have mostly covered. So, by working on solutions for illnesses covered by vaccines, the lesser dependence on vaccines can be offset by good alternatives in many cases. Please note that the leading cause of death in the end is from an illness leading to Pneumonia. There are three types of Pneumonia, and these are links for review. The links are:

Chapter 3 Other Changes to the Medical Industry

1. Measles And Other Viruses – Giant Cell Pneumonia: See **Hyperlink Reference Table 3.8-1 GIANT CELL PNEUMONIA: Clinicopathologic and Experimental Studies** below.
2. Bordetella Pertussis bacterial toxins leading to lung infection causing Pneumonia: See **Hyperlink Reference Table 3.8-2 Whooping Cough (Pertussis) in Adults** below.
3. Chickenpox - Varicella Pneumonia: See **Hyperlink Reference Table 3.8-3 Varicella pneumonia** below.

*Table 5- Hyperlink Reference Table 3.8-1 GIANT CELL PNEUMONIA: Clinicopathologic and Experimental Studies*

https://publications.aap.org/pediatrics/article-abstract/18/6/888/29059/GIANT-CELL-PNEUMONIA-Clinicopathologic-and?redirectedFrom=fulltext

| **See the Hyperlink above this table.** | Google search: measles giant cell pneumonia experimental aap |
|---|---|
| Title: GIANT CELL PNEUMONIA: Clinicopathologic and Experimental Studies | Authors: J. M. Adams; D. T. Imagawa; Miye Yoshimori; R. W. Huntington |

| | Published Online 12/1/1956 |
|---|---|
| **Book Summary of Link: The article must have been initially a print copy.**<br><br>**The type of Pneumonia associated with Measles is Giant Cell Pneumonia.** | Quoted Text: "In two fatal cases of measles the major pathologic finding was a pneumonia characterized principally by giant cells and inclusion bodies. The pattern was not dissimilar to that encountered in two cases of "primary pneumonitis with inclusion bodies," evidently not due to measles. The development of giant cells has been illustrated in tissue cultures infected with adenoviruses and measles viruses, and in ferrets infected with distemper viruses. Conspicuous giant cell production in the lung appears to be a rather general viral phenomenon, not peculiar to any one virus." |

Chapter 3 Other Changes to the Medical Industry

*Table 6- Hyperlink Reference Table 3.8-2 Whooping Cough (Pertussis) in Adults*

| https://www.hopkinsmedicine.org/health/conditions-and-diseases/whooping-cough-pertussis-in-adults | Google search: John Hopkins Pertussis |
|---|---|
| Title: Whooping Cough (Pertussis) in Adults | Authors: John Hopkins Hospital<br><br>Published Online and date not shown |
| **Book Summary of Link: I have not found a separate type of Pneumonia associated with bad Pertussis cases that lead to Pneumonia.**<br><br>**I suspect that the type of Pneumonia here in the case of Bordetella Pertussis is some non-Pneumococcal Pneumonia, probably caused by a separate Pneumonia toxin in the Bordetella Pertussis bacteria.**<br><br>**It is also possible that in some cases of Bordetella Pertussis infections, a** | Quoted Text: "Whooping cough can last up to 10 weeks and can lead to pneumonia and other complications." |

| | |
|---|---|
| case of Pneumococcal Pneumonia comes into effect. | |

*Table 7- Hyperlink Reference Table 3.8-3 Varicella pneumonia*

https://radiopaedia.org/articles/varicella-pneumonia?lang=us#:~:text=Varicella%20pneumonia%20is%20a%20type,significant%20complications%20including%20varicella%20pneumonia.

| **See the Hyperlink above this table.** | Google search: Radiopaedia varicella-pneumonia |
|---|---|
| Title: Varicella pneumonia | Authors: Sonam Vadera<br><br>Published Online 6/21/2021 |
| **Book Summary of Link: Varicella Pneumonia can come from other similar viruses other than Chicken Pox.** | Quoted Text: "**Varicella pneumonia** is a type of viral pneumonia. It is a common cause of multiple small round calcific lung lesions. Varicella-zoster virus most commonly causes self-limited benign disease (chickenpox) in children. However, in adults it tends to cause significant complications including varicella pneumonia." |

Chapter 3 Other Changes to the Medical Industry

# Chapter 4 Other Work to Improve the Overall Health of All at a Reduced Cost

## 4.0 Key Related Points

- **There is a lot of potential improvement in the federal government of the United States.**
- **Much of the improvement here in this book can be a joint effort to improve the financial position of the lower and middle classes plus the budget of the United States**

- **Many of the improvements can also improve the health of the people of the United States and the world.**
- **I don't believe in trickle-down economics; I am more of a trickle-up economist.**

## 4.1 More Exercise

We should establish more robust guidelines for exercise by all people and build more significant online exercise group networks. I suggest establishing daily routine activities that interact with AI cell phone and other apps to track adequate exercise activities. The apps should also keep track of activity and blood pressure and other related stats.

I also suggest providing federal tax incentives to offset various small expenses by individuals for the cost of gym plans and other exercise activities.

## 4.2 Natural Food Infrastructure Alternatives and Changes to Pharmacies

I researched by asking a group for input on natural food ideas and added some general ideas. Some input was for more small farms to be kept as part of our society, less or no use of Genetically modified

Chapter 4 Other Work to Improve the Overall Health of All at a Reduced Cost

Organisms (GMOs) in food, and more use of "real food."

There is the idea of dramatically changing local pharmacies, where they don't sell, provide, or distribute vaccines anymore and replace existing food sections with natural ones.

Local pharmacies, big box stores like Walmart, and big supermarkets could be great candidates for selling and distributing more natural food alternatives. We could have many natural food coops that coordinate with natural food enthusiasts, set up, and engage people in choosing natural food alternatives for availability and distribution out of several businesses that are local to most people. I would also like to see more vegetable options in restaurants.

A half pharmacy/half natural food sales and distribution business could replace Walgreens. And the same kind of natural food coop idea could be associated with the new alternative to Walgreens. One could also insist that this new or alternate business would not sell any food that is not "natural." All of the food would be organic or "natural." The latest business format would have kiosks for convenient processing of certain parts of the business.

And one thing related to natural foods would be a whole line of natural drinks with much less sugar and no unhealthy sugar substitutes.

Chapter 4 Other Work to Improve the Overall Health of All at a Reduced Cost

# 4.3 Lower Cost Medical Services For Individuals Without Medical Insurance

The government should provide cost-control services to individuals to control the costs of medical services for the uninsured or underinsured. We should not have a system emphasizing having or needing costly medical insurance.

It should be illegal for medical providers to charge more for medical services for the uninsured or under-insured than what is paid for by insurance companies and the government.

We should work to reduce costs for all medical services in general by other means.

# Chapter 5 Other Major Federal Budgetary Improvement Efforts

## 5.0 Key Related Points

- The war in Ukraine shows dramatic improvements in defensive warfare capability. These new techniques should be used to reduce the cost of the federal defense budget.
- We need to see what the new Trump administration will do regarding improvements in the federal budget, if any.
- This chapter adds to what is being billed as a $2 trillion yearly reduction in the federal budget. My added $3

**trillion per year ideas augment and depend on that $2 trillion per year thinking.**

# 5.1 Introductory Comments

My book here adds to the plans of the upcoming 2025 presidential administration.

The Cato Institute, a libertarian think tank based in Washington, D.C., plans to cut the federal budget by $2 trillion annually. The Cato Report is the basis for the newly proposed US Federal Department of Government Efficiency. See the reference and some key details of the report in **Hyperlink Reference Table 5.1-1 Cato Report for the Department of Government Efficiency (DOGE): How to Downsize and Reform Government**.

*Table 8- Hyperlink Reference Table 5.1-1 Cato Report for the Department of Government Efficiency (DOGE): How to Downsize and Reform Government*

| |
|---|
| https://www.cato.org/blog/catos-report-department-government-efficiency-doge |
| Google Search: DOGE Cato Report |

| |
|---|
| Title: Cato Report for the Department of Government Efficiency (DOGE): How to Downsize and Reform Government |
| Authors: Alex Nowrasteh and Ryan Bourne, Published Online 12/11/24 |
| **Book Summary of Link: This is the basis for the Trump GOP administration's plans to work with the DOGE team.** |
| Quoted Text: <u>Chapter 1</u> describes cuts and reforms to the *Bureaucracy and the Administrative State*, such as eliminating DEI programs, affirmative action, and collection of race data; ... <br> <u>Chapter 2</u> details cuts to *Regulation* that would reduce costly overreach and boost economic performance. Those supply-side reforms should focus on energy production, environmental rules, the financial sector, health care, childcare, and the Jones Act and similar laws. <br><br> <u>Chapter 3</u> proposes numerous *Spending Cuts and Tax Reforms*, such as ending aid to states and subsidies for politically favored sectors of the economy, sharply reducing federal involvement in education, streamlining national security spending, reining in emergency spending, and reforming entitlements. |

Chapter 5 Other Major Federal Budgetary Improvement Efforts

# 5.2 Defense Industry Changes

The defense industry is somewhat expensive because of big-ticket items like planes, submarines, etc. I suggest working on newer, lower-cost technology as a substitute for high-ticket items like more drones. There should also be a review of how to get more bang for the federal budget dollar straight across the board for defense.

# 5.3 Other Federal Discretionary Budget Changes Plus Other Changes

Elon Musk and others on the presidential transition team are working on a $2 trillion spending reduction plan. I don't know how well they will do with those plans. I also figured that they plan on medical cuts and have considered that in my $800 billion plan for cutting medical costs for the government and all individuals. I figure they will only get about $200 billion in cuts in the medical field without making a more dramatic set of changes, as I have outlined in this book.

# 5.4 Book Summary

My proposed ideas are highly dependent on the new 2025 presidential administration's implementing their planned cuts and taking up ideas like those outlined in this book. We will see how things progress. The ideas are mostly related to dramatic cuts in payouts to the medical industry and lower costs for individuals and corporations paying for health insurance plans for workers.

**This is the second book I have written about opportunities related to trillions of dollars. My first book is titled "Vaccines—Scientific Analysis—And the $7.8 Trillion Per Year Economic Opportunity for the United States: A Strategy and Reference Book R3." It can be found on Amazon.com by searching for $7.8 trillion or Karl Guenther. This other book is much more technical and substantial.**

I also like increasing taxes on billionaires to about $800 billion per year to eliminate the annual federal budget deficits and work towards reducing the long-term debt of the US federal government, which was done twice in our history.

In times of large federal debt, the top tax rate for high earners went up to levels in the low 90% range. I am not suggesting that top tax rates should be that high, but that there should be much higher top tax rates and real minimum tax rates on billionaires. This part of my thinking also helps to fill any gap that the government can't work in the overall $3 trillion plan.

I would also like to see some relatively small but essential tax cuts on those earning less than $50,000 per year as an individual or $100,000 as a married couple. Primarily, I would like the tax on social

Chapter 5 Other Major Federal Budgetary Improvement Efforts

security income to be adjusted for inflation every year, and I would like to see a one-time increase in the standard deduction of about 30%.

Chapter 5 Other Major Federal Budgetary Improvement Efforts

# Index

## Index Entries

Made in the USA
Middletown, DE
04 February 2025

70131872R00029